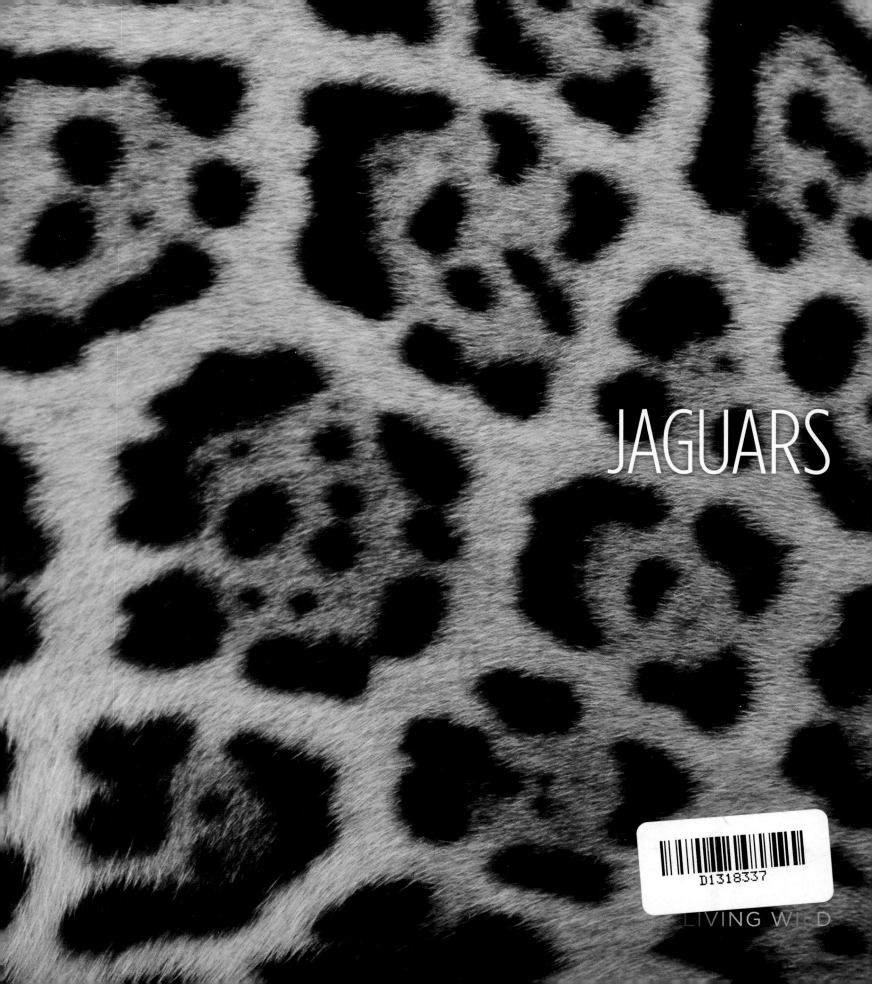

JAGUARS

LIVING WILD

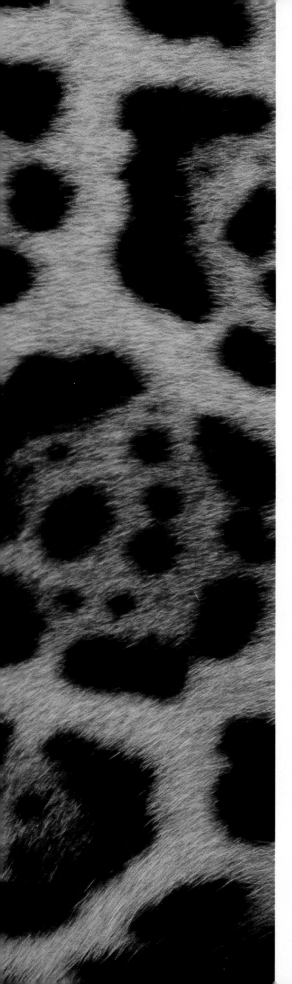

LIVING WILD

Published by Creative Paperbacks
P.O. Box 227, Mankato, Minnesota 56002
Creative Paperbacks is an imprint of The Creative Company
www.thecreativecompany.us

Design and production by Mary Herrmann
Art direction by Rita Marshall
Printed by Corporate Graphics in the United States of America

Photographs by 123RF (Pierrette Guertin, Paul Hampton), Alamy (Danita Delimont, Frans Lanting Studio, Jack Sullivan), Corbis (Tom Brakefield, Michael & Patricia Fogden, Frans Lanting, Kennan Ward), Dreamstime (Baronoskie, Stef Bennett, Casey Bishop, Gary Bryant, David Davis, Anthony Hathaway, Jesus Eloy Ramos Lara, David Leindecker, Johnny Lye, Christopher Moncrieff, Sharon Morris), Getty Images (Nick Gordon, Henri J. F. Rousseau, Joel Sartore, Steve Winter), iStockphoto (Paula Connelly, go1xm, Ken Klotz, Jason Pacheco, Evelyn Peyton, Mariann Rea, Windzepher)

The Library of Congress has cataloged the hardcover edition as follows:
Gish, Melissa.
Jaguars / by Melissa Gish.
p. cm. — (Living wild)
Includes bibliographical references and index.
Summary: A look at jaguars, including their habitats, physical characteristics such as their powerful jaws, behaviors, relationships with humans, and threatened status in the world today.
ISBN 978-1-60818-079-0 (hardcover)
ISBN 978-0-89812-671-6 (pbk)
1. Jaguar—Juvenile literature. I. Title.

QL737.C23G515 2011
599.75'5—dc22   2010028315

CPSIA: 110310 PO1385

First Edition
9 8 7 6 5 4 3 2 1

JAGUARS

Melissa Gish

On a misty summer morning before sunrise, a jaguar creeps silently along a marshy

path near the Madeira River in east-central Brazil.

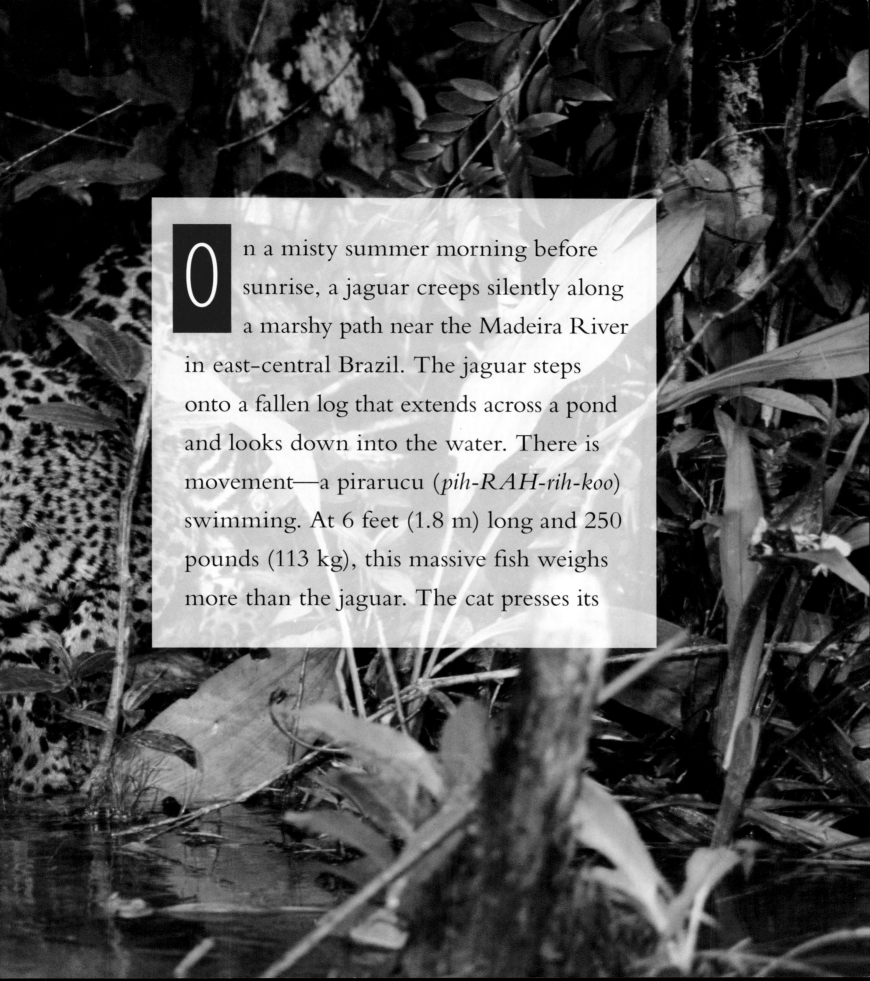

On a misty summer morning before sunrise, a jaguar creeps silently along a marshy path near the Madeira River in east-central Brazil. The jaguar steps onto a fallen log that extends across a pond and looks down into the water. There is movement—a pirarucu (*pih-RAH-rih-koo*) swimming. At 6 feet (1.8 m) long and 250 pounds (113 kg), this massive fish weighs more than the jaguar. The cat presses its

body against the log, tenses its hind legs, and tilts its tail to provide perfect balance. Then it leaps into the water and lands on the fish, instantly clamping its jaws down on the skull of its prey. The fish struggles, but it cannot break free of the jaguar's death grip. The big cat drags its meal to shore and disappears with it into the wetland forest, on its way to deliver the fresh pirarucu to its young.

WHERE IN THE WORLD THEY LIVE

The single species of jaguar is found only in the Americas. Its range extends mainly from Mexico, through Central America, and as far south as Paraguay and Argentina in South America. A very small number of the big cats live in the southwestern United States, particularly in Arizona, but the animals are rarely seen there. The colored squares represent locations along its known range.

■ **Jaguar**
Mexico,
Central and
South America

SILENT BUT DEADLY

The jaguar is the third-largest of the world's four species of big cats. Its closest relatives, the lions of Africa and India and the tigers of Asia, are larger, and the leopards of Africa and Asia are smaller. All cats typically growl, screech, and scream, but lions, tigers, leopards, and jaguars all roar. The jaguar's roar sounds like a scratchy cough, and the cat roars to warn other jaguars of its presence. Once widespread across North America from coast to coast, the jaguar is now rarely seen in the United States. This solitary cat can be found in Mexico and Central and South America. It prefers dense rainforests, where it can hide from its only predator, humans, but it can also survive in dry grasslands and deserts, as long as water is nearby.

The big cats are members of the Felidae family and the genus *Panthera*, which refers to the word "panther," a word used to describe leopards, cougars (or pumas), and jaguars in different parts of the world. The jaguar's scientific name is *Panthera onca*. In Greek, the word *pan* means "all," and *ther* means "beast," making the jaguar a beast that hunts all other animals. The word *onca*

Male lions can weigh up to 550 pounds (249 kg)—more than twice as much as the largest jaguar.

Jaguars are known by different names in different countries: *jaguareté* in Paraguay, *otorongo* in Peru, and *yaguar* in Venezuela.

Jaguars have a bite force of 1,800 pounds of pressure per square inch (126 kg/cm²)—almost 10 times stronger than that of a human.

means "hook," which refers to the jaguar's sharp claws. The word "jaguar" comes from the language of the Tupinamba, an **indigenous** people of Brazil who lived south of the Amazon River. Their word *yaguara* translates to "the beast that kills with one leap."

While scientists currently accept that there is only one species of jaguar, three subspecies are defined according to their geographical locations. The northernmost subspecies of jaguar, located primarily in Mexico and Central America, is the smallest. The centrally located jaguars, found throughout the Amazon region, are larger. Jaguars found as far south as northeastern Argentina have the largest body size. Scientists speculate that variations in the sizes of available prey have influenced the **evolution** of jaguars. The farther south they are from Mexico, the larger their prey becomes.

Fewer than 1,000 jaguars exist in Mexico and Central America, and roughly the same number can be found in the wetlands of northern Brazil. About 200 survive in Argentina. The largest population, about 15,000 individuals, resides in the Amazon Rainforest. The number of jaguars in the world continues to decline due to habitat destruction and **poaching**. Approximately 120

Like all cats, jaguars have scent glands on their cheeks and between their toes that are used to mark territory.

A jaguar uses its 12-inch (30.5 cm) tongue like sand-paper to scrape bits of flesh from an animal's bone.

jaguars are protected in zoos throughout North America.

Jaguars are muscular animals with short, powerful legs and broad, rounded feet, making them silent stalkers and expert climbers, leapers, and swimmers. Male jaguars weigh about 120 pounds (54 kg) in Mexico and Central America and up to 220 pounds (100 kg) in their South American wetland habitats. They stand about 3 feet (91 cm) tall at the shoulder and can grow to be 8.5 feet (2.6 m) long when their 30-inch (76.2 cm) tail is included. Females are typically 10 to 20 percent smaller than males. Lighter jaguars are capable of hunting in trees, where they attack monkeys, as well as on the ground, but heavier cats tend to stay out of the trees.

In order to crush the armored shells of turtles and armadillos, which are plentiful prey, jaguars developed massive, heavy skulls and the most powerful teeth and jaws of all big cats. Their upper canine teeth can be more than half an inch (1.3 cm) wide and as long as an adult human's index finger. Their gums are equipped with pressure-sensitive nerves that tell the jaguar exactly how to position its teeth for the deadliest bite. While other big cats generally crush a prey animal's throat to cut off

Hilaire's side-necked turtle is found in ponds and swamps near the southern-most part of the jaguar's range.

its air supply, the jaguar's method involves biting through the skull to fatally pierce the brain and spinal cord. To aid in efficiently devouring their meals, jaguars have sharp projections, called papillae, on their tongues that they use like a grater to scrape meat and marrow from bones.

Jaguars vary in color from golden yellow to reddish-brown. The black, ringed markings on a jaguar's fur are called rosettes because their shape resembles rose blossoms. The jaguar may be mistaken for the similarly spotted leopard or cheetah, but the spots actually differentiate between the species. Leopard rosettes are black with brown or golden centers, and cheetah spots are solid black, while jaguars' black rosettes contain lines and spots inside them. No two jaguars have the same markings. Like human fingerprints, each jaguar's rosettes are unique.

The jaguar's coloration provides **camouflage**. In rainforest habitats, the jaguar's dense spots blend in with the leaves, stones, and other materials that litter the forest floor. The jaguar's golden fur resembles the flashes of light that occur as sunlight penetrates the shadowy darkness and shines through the grasses of the jaguar's habitat. At night, the rosettes help the animal blend into the moonlit darkness.

Jaguars' dark rosettes have broken, irregular borders, unlike the solid outlines of leopards and cheetahs'.

Domestic cats can purr when breathing in and out, but jaguars and other roaring cats can purr only when breathing out.

Some jaguars are melanistic—black-colored—and known as black panthers. Melanism is inherited and can occur in all cats. It is caused when the body produces increased amounts of melanin, the chemical in living things that causes dark-colored cells to form. About six percent of all jaguars are born melanistic, but they still have rosettes, just like other jaguars. In certain lighting conditions, the markings become visible. However, at night, these jaguars become practically invisible, making them especially deadly hunters.

Jaguars tend to rest during the day and stay awake much of the night. They are crepuscular animals, which means that they are most active during the twilight hours of dawn and dusk. With good night vision, jaguars are able to see in near darkness. The jaguar's eyes are equipped with a reflective layer of tissue called a tapetum lucidum. This tissue collects light and concentrates it in the center of the retina, the light-sensitive part of the inner eye, allowing the jaguar to see twice as well in low light as it can in daylight. The tissue also causes eyeshine, making the eyes reflect color when a light is shined on them. The jaguar's eyeshine is a bright yellow-orange in color.

Melanism occurs in jaguars of Central and South America, but no black panthers have been documented in Mexico.

Remote cameras have sighted as many as 1,000 jaguars in Bolivia's Kaa-Iya del Gran Chaco National Park.

SPOTS IN THE JUNGLE

The jaguar is a solitary animal, living alone in a particular area called its home range. The size of a male jaguar's home range varies from 20 square miles (52 sq km) to around 53 square miles (137 sq km), depending on how many jaguars exist in a region. A female's home range is smaller, between 10 square miles (26 sq km) and 37 square miles (96 sq km). Unlike most cat species, jaguars love the water. Their home ranges typically include access to rivers, streams, or smaller pools and ponds, where jaguars may spend hours soaking. A male may allow a certain number of females' home ranges to overlap into his home range, but he will defend his territory against intruding male jaguars.

Jaguars spend about half of their time actively roaming their territories, keeping their boundaries secure. A jaguar marks its boundaries by spraying urine and making deep scratches on trees. It will also roar to announce its presence to potential rivals. Hunting is a relatively small part of a jaguar's day and usually takes place very early in the morning or at dusk. Studies have revealed that jaguars regularly prey on 85 different species of creatures. Jaguars are considered

Jaguars rarely attack humans, but they have been known to stalk people as a way of "escorting" them out of their territories.

apex predators, meaning they are at the top of the **food chain**. The cats also contribute to the health of their communities by preying on sick, injured, and old animals. They are not fussy eaters but opportunistic feeders, meaning they will eat any kind of prey that happens to be nearby.

Jaguars hunt both large and small prey. Capybaras, which resemble giant guinea pigs and are the largest rodents on Earth, and tapirs, which are piglike **mammals** that typically weigh from 500 to 700 pounds (227–318 kg), are favorite large meals. Aquatic creatures, including turtles, fish, and caimans—the smallest members of the

crocodile family—make satisfying smaller meals. Jaguars will sometimes even snatch monkeys from trees. Nothing is too small for a snack.

The jaguar is more similar to the leopard than it is to its African relative the cheetah, a cat built for speed and endurance as it chases its prey. Leopards and jaguars are built for launching surprise attacks instead. They are capable of sprinting quickly but are seldom required to do so, as they choose to sneak up on their prey. These cats have thick pads on the bottoms of their feet that provide a cushion as they creep silently toward prey before pouncing,

Like its relative the tiger, the jaguar has no fear of water and will chase prey into rivers and lakes.

While melanism is a characteristic passed through relatives, it may skip an entire generation or several litters of cubs.

and they can leap as far as 20 feet (6 m) in a single bound.

Jaguars typically avoid one another except during courtship and mating. Females reach maturity at age two and males at age three or four. When she is ready to mate, a female will leave her home range and seek out suitable males, who make mewing cries (similar to those produced by small cats) to attract her attention.

Jaguars can mate at any time of the year. Each mating period lasts for 6 to 17 days. Once a female has consented to mate, the male bites the back of the female's neck to stimulate the release of an egg, which he then fertilizes. The female may mate with more than one male before returning to her home range, resulting in her having a litter of cubs who will potentially have different fathers. Before she gives birth, the female jaguar selects a secluded den site—a protected place such as underneath a stand of thick, thorny brush or in a tangle of tree roots—where she and her offspring will be safest from predators. After 93 to 110 days, the female gives birth. Jaguars usually have two cubs, but up to four cubs may be born in rare instances.

Cubs weigh only about 1.6 pounds (726 g) at birth. When cubs are born, the spots on their coats are very

Despite the sea turtle's endangered status, people are not allowed to protect them from jaguar attacks.

Over the past decade, more jaguars have been driven to hunt near the ocean, snatching sea turtles from the beaches.

The papillae on a jaguar's tongue work like dozens of little cups to collect water when the cat drinks.

close together, making their fur appear a solid brownish color. They have light-colored eyes that do not open until the cubs are 14 days old. As cubs grow, their eyes will darken to a golden brown, and the spots on their coats will spread out. They make bleating and mewing sounds to stay in contact with their mother, and as they become more playful, they practice their roaring, which sounds more like chirping until the cubs are nearly a year old.

Cubs rely on their mother's milk for nourishment for the first 5 to 6 months of their lives, but as soon as 10 weeks after birth, their mother will introduce them to meat, bringing prey home to the den for the cubs to eat. When the cubs are about six months old, they will begin to join their mother on hunts. This can be dangerous business, and the **mortality rate** for cubs is high. The greatest threats to young jaguars are constricting snakes, such as the anaconda, which may lie in wait for a cub to enter the water and then suddenly wrap itself around the surprised jaguar, suffocating it before devouring it whole.

By the time they are one year old, jaguar cubs are fully grown and can fend for themselves, yet it takes time for young jaguars to fine-tune their hunting skills. They

continue to hunt with their mother, learning from her and sharing kills with her, until they are at least two years old. The fully trained young jaguars then set out alone in search of home ranges that have not yet been claimed or that have been abandoned by other jaguars. A female cub may be allowed to take a portion of her mother's home range and make it her own, but males must move away so they will not be in competition with older males in the area.

Because jaguars are difficult to monitor, it is not known for certain how long these elusive cats can live in the wild. Some studies suggest that jaguars survive no more than 12 to 15 years. But in captivity, jaguars may live almost 25 years.

Jaguar cubs are born with sharp claws, which they practice using while playing to develop their hunting skills.

The image of a jaguar eating a heart was carved on a stone column at the Mayan city of Chichen Itza.

CREATURE OF TWO WORLDS

The jaguar is perhaps the most important mammal in the **cultural** history of the indigenous peoples of Mesoamerica, an area from central Mexico south into Central America. Archaeologists have discovered a wide range of artifacts depicting the jaguar in various forms. Revered—but also feared—for its stealth and strength, the jaguar was considered both a god and a demon. And because the jaguar is at home in both the water and the trees, early cultures associated the jaguar with the ability to travel between Earth, represented by the water, and the spirit world, represented by the tall rainforest trees.

In many ancient cultures, men called shamans were thought to have influence in the spirit world. They performed religious ceremonies to tell the future, used herbal medicines to cure illness, and communicated with spirits to obtain advice for their tribes' ruling elders. Shamans were highly respected, and in Mesoamerican cultures such as the Olmec, Mayan, and Aztec societies, equally respected was the jaguar, which was closely tied to shamanism.

While jaguars are not endangered worldwide, scientists believe their populations have decreased by as much as 50 percent in the last 100 years.

A jaguar mask is used in traditional Mexican dances in which humans hunt and capture a jaguar to express power.

The ancient Olmecs, who built cities along the coast of the Gulf of Mexico from about 1400 to 400 B.C., believed that jaguars had special relationships with shamans. The jaguar was thought to be a companion animal, or *nagual*, whose job was to protect shamans as they performed their supernatural rituals. The Olmecs also believed that shamans could transform themselves into jaguars. Ancient artifacts such as engravings and **fetishes** depict this transformation.

In Mayan **mythology**, the jaguar was associated with a vast collection of deities and spiritual beings called *Balam*, which were believed to protect people from danger. The Maya, whose civilization began around 2000 B.C. and continued until the Spanish invasions of the late 1400s A.D., believed that the dark-colored Jaguar God of the Underworld and the light-colored Jaguar God of the Upper World worked with the Creator to construct the universe and then continued to watch over the living and the dead. Maya people also believed that humans and jaguars shared power over the land and all of its creatures. Much of their artwork and many common objects, from wall murals to etched pottery and tools, that survive depict this relationship.

The Maya were also known for the elaborate ceremonial

The Aztecs, another group of people native to what is today Mexico, made stone containers that looked like jaguars.

This 1895 painting of the famous Aztec king Montezuma is on display at the National Art Museum in Mexico City.

clothing worn by their kings, which included jaguar **pelts** and helmets made in the shape of jaguars' heads. Many rulers also associated themselves with the jaguar's power by giving themselves names such as Jaguar Paw, Moon Jaguar, and Bird Jaguar. Courageous warriors also wore jaguar pelts and adornments made of jaguar claws and teeth to symbolize the jaguar's strength and powerful spirit.

From the 1300s until the early 1500s A.D., the Aztec Empire spread throughout central Mexico. Its most powerful tribe, the Mexica, lived in the city of Tenochtitlan, and the people embraced the jaguar as a major spiritual being. They believed that Tezcatlipoca, the god of darkness and night, could transform into a jaguar, called *ocelotl* in their language. Then he could travel silently in the darkness and be disguised with spots like stars in the night sky.

The Aztecs were known for sacrificing humans to appease their gods and strike fear into their enemies. They used a special container in the shape of a jaguar, called an *ocelotl-cuauhxicalli*, to store the hearts of their sacrificed victims. The practice was associated with the earth and the underworld, of which the jaguar was considered an integral part. Aztec kings also wore jaguar pelts, and the two highest military forces in Aztec culture were the Order of the Eagle and the Order of the Jaguar. Only men of noble birth could belong to these two orders.

Historians believe that the first pictures of jaguars to be drawn by Europeans were based on jaguars kept in captivity in the palace of Tenochtitlan's king Moctezuma

The ancient city of Teotihuacan, known for its pyramids, predated the Aztecs' Tenochtitlan by about 1,500 years.

II (also known as Montezuma), who ruled in the early 1500s during the time of the Spanish invasion of the Aztec Empire.

Considering its long history of being respected and feared for its strength and hunting skill, it is no wonder that the jaguar has remained an important figure today. The jaguar is the unofficial national symbol of the South American country of Brazil, where the indigenous peoples have long used the fat from jaguars to make some traditional medicines, and of Brazil's neighbor Guyana, where jaguars are respected as bringers of new life. Guyana's **coat of arms** includes one jaguar holding an ax and another holding a sugar cane and a stalk of rice to symbolize the nation's mining and agricultural industries.

Jaguars also represent a number of sports teams in North and South America. The Jacksonville Jaguars joined the National Football League in 1995. The team logo is a roaring jaguar's head, and its mascot is Jaxson de Ville, or Jax, who makes special appearances around the country to entertain fans with his crazy antics. At the collegiate level, the Jaguars represent the University of South Alabama, located in the city of Mobile. In 2009, the university's football team went undefeated, living up to the spirit of its logo, a fiercely roaring jaguar.

In 1968, Mexico City chose the jaguar as its unofficial mascot for the 1968 Summer Olympics because of the animal's symbolic value to traditional Mexican culture. Inspired by the popularity of Mexico City's jaguar, the Olympics began using official mascots in 1972. To this day, the jaguar remains a valued symbol in Mexican sports. The Chiapas Jaguars (Jaguares de Chiapas) are based in Mexico's southernmost state and represent Chiapas in the national professional soccer league. The team colors are gold and black—mimicking the coloration of real jaguars.

The strength and speed of the jaguar is what car enthusiasts consider when they look at a Jaguar automobile. First created in 1935, the Jaguar line of cars is well known for luxury and high performance. Until 1998, Jaguar's XJ220 held the world speed record for a mass-produced automobile, reaching a top speed of 217 miles (349 km) per hour. Jaguar's mascot, a silver jaguar frozen in mid-leap, captures the essence of this magnificent wild cat.

Jaguar hood ornaments are sought after by those who enjoy the hobby of collecting such automobile mascots.

When the sun begins to set, a jaguar will patrol its territory to search for food and to warn off intruders.

hunt—on their land. In many portions of the Pantanal, as well as other private land all across Central and South America, the overhunting of deer, peccaries, and other types of jaguar prey has led to a decline of these species, forcing jaguars to go after larger yet more available food sources—namely, cattle.

When a jaguar repeatedly hunts livestock, it may be considered a **nuisance** animal, and while the killing of jaguars is illegal everywhere in the Americas except in

Hunters Jack Childs and Werner Glen photographed two jaguars in Arizona in 1996, prompting further jaguar research in the U.S.

I SAW A HOLE IN THE MAN

And a Man sat alone...

Drenched deep in sadness

And all the animals drew near to him and said:

"We do not like to see you so sad

Ask us for whatever you wish and you shall have it."

The Man said: "I want to have good sight."

The Vulture replied: "You shall have mine."

The Man said: "I want to be strong."

The Jaguar said: "You shall be strong like me."

The Man said: "I long to know the secrets of the earth."

The Serpent replied: "I will show them to you."

And so it went with all the animals.

And when the Man had all the gifts they could give; he left.

Then the Owl said to the other animals:

"Now the Man knows much and is able to do many things.

Suddenly I am afraid."

The Deer said: "The Man has all that he needs.

Now his sadness will stop."

But the Owl replied: "No. I saw a hole in the Man.

Deep like a hunger he will never fill.

It is what makes him sad and what makes him want.

He will go on taking and taking.

Until one day the world will say:

I am no more and I have nothing left to give."

Mayan Fable

Ecuador, Guyana, and Bolivia (where limited trophy hunting is allowed), nuisance animals can be killed in order to protect livestock. Many ranchers do not give jaguars a second chance after they have killed once and will shoot the big cats on sight. Such aggression toward jaguars has contributed to their being classified as a near threatened species by the International Union for Conservation of Nature (IUCN).

Jaguars are also in jeopardy because of **deforestation** caused by logging, mining, and agriculture, which fragments their habitats into small sections, cutting them off from certain food sources and limiting mating options. Poaching is yet another problem. Though not as serious as it was in the first half of the 20th century, when more than 18,000 jaguars were killed each year for their beautiful pelts, the illegal slaughter and trade of jaguars still occurs.

The jaguar is one of the world's most stunning creatures. As a large predator, it is vital to the health of its rainforest community. Researchers have only begun to uncover the mysteries of the jaguar, an amazing cat with more secrets to reveal—if only it can survive human interference long enough.

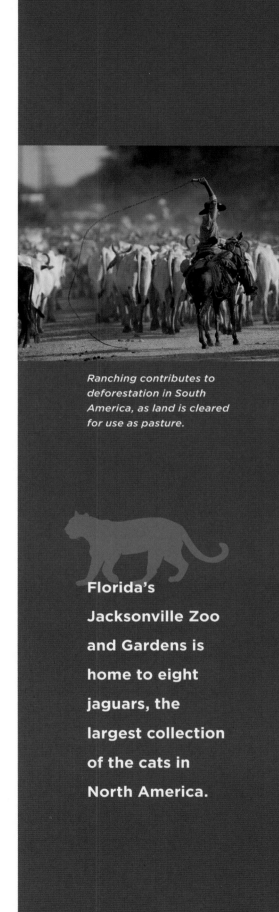

Ranching contributes to deforestation in South America, as land is cleared for use as pasture.

Florida's Jacksonville Zoo and Gardens is home to eight jaguars, the largest collection of the cats in North America.

ANIMAL TALE:
THE STORY OF JAGUAR MAN

The people of the Amazon Basin believe the jaguar possesses great powers. This story from Brazil tells why the jaguar hides his secrets in the rainforest.

There was once a boy named Uaica who lived with his grandfather in a village. Because he was small and weak, Uaica was often bullied by the other boys. Uaica would go into the rainforest to escape his tormentors. One day, as he was walking in the forest he came upon an old man.

"I am Sina-a, child of Jaguar," said the old man.

Uaica had heard of Sina-a, or Jaguar Man. He was said to be a great teacher.

"Come," Jaguar Man instructed Uaica.

Uaica listened as Jaguar Man told wonderful stories about how he secretly cared for all humans, creating plants for them to eat, bringing them game, and ruling the night to keep them safe. Uiaca learned many things from Jaguar Man, who made him promise to tell no one of their meeting.

Day after day, Uaica returned to the forest to listen to Jaguar Man, who was a great shaman, and to learn his magic.

One day, Uaica could no longer contain his excitement and told his grandfather about Jaguar Man. "This is great power that Jaguar Man has bestowed upon you," the boy's grandfather said. "He must believe that you have goodness in your heart so that you will not use this power for evil."

This turned out to be true, for soon one of the boys in the village became very ill and everyone believed he would die. Uaica knew the boy as one of his worst

tormentors, but he went to the boy anyway and cured him using the power of magical healing that Jaguar Man had taught him.

That night, Jaguar Man appeared to Uaica in a dream. "You passed the test," he said to the boy. "You showed goodness toward your enemy. Now I can rest, and you can become Jaguar Man. Your path will be a lonely one, but you will take over the care for your people."

Uaica was grateful for Jaguar Man's teachings and began to care for the people in his village, healing them of their sicknesses and creating beautiful artifacts from shells, nuts, and feathers. He wondered why Jaguar Man had said he would be lonely.

And then he learned why. Some of the people did not appreciate Uaica's gifts. They grew envious. "Why should you have the power of healing and the skill of art when we do not?" they asked. In their jealousy, they plotted to kill Uaica.

One night, while Uaica and his grandfather sat down to share a meal, the assassins crept up behind Uaica with heavy clubs. Just as one man raised his club, Uaica turned around to face him. "I am now a powerful shaman," said Uaica, "capable of seeing behind me without turning around." The would-be attackers ran away.

Then Uaica went to the village elders. "I am not wanted," Uaica said, "so I must go away." The elders were saddened as they watched Uaica disappear into the night. Like the jaguar, he remains hidden alone in the rainforest to this day, appearing only to people who, with goodness in their hearts, ask to receive Jaguar Man's healing wisdom.

Henri Rousseau

GLOSSARY

camouflage – the ability to hide, due to coloring or markings that blend in with a given environment

coat of arms – the official symbol of a family, state, nation, or other group

cultural – of or relating to particular groups in a society that share behaviors and characteristics that are accepted as normal by that group

deforestation – the clearing away of trees from a forest

evolution – the process of gradually developing into a new form

fetishes – objects believed by certain cultures to embody spirits or possess magical powers

food chain – a system in nature in which living things are dependent on each other for food

Global Positioning System – a system of satellites, computers, and other electronic devices that work together to determine the location of objects or living things that carry a trackable device

indigenous – originating in a particular region or country

land bridge – a piece of land connecting two landmasses that allowed people and animals to pass from one place to another

mammals – warm-blooded animals that have a backbone and hair or fur, give birth to live young, and produce milk to feed their young

marsupials – mammals whose young are born early and further develop in a pouch on the mother's body

mortality rate – the number of deaths in a certain area or period

mythology – a collection of myths, or popular, traditional beliefs or stories that explain how something came to be or that are associated with a person or object

nuisance – something annoying or harmful to people or the land

pelts – the skins of animals with the fur or wool still attached

poaching – hunting protected species of wild animals, even though doing so is against the law

radio collar – a collar fitted with a small electronic device that sends a signal to a radio receiver

satellites – mechanical devices launched into space; they may be designed to travel around Earth or toward other planets or the sun

SELECTED BIBLIOGRAPHY

Arizona Game and Fish Department. "Jaguar Conservation." Jaguar Conservation Team. http://www.azgfd.gov/w_c/es/jaguar_management.shtml.

Brown, David E. *Borderland Jaguars: Tigres de la Frontera.* Salt Lake City: University of Utah Press, 2001.

Churchill, Kate. *In Search of the Jaguar.* DVD. Washington, D.C.: National Geographic Society, 2006.

Jaguar Species Survival Plan. "Jaguar Fact Sheet." American Zoo and Aquarium Association. http://www.jaguarssp.org/jagFactSheet.htm.

Mahler, Richard. *The Jaguar's Shadow: Searching for a Mythic Cat.* New Haven, Conn.: Yale University Press, 2009.

Rabinowitz, Alan. *Jaguar: One Man's Struggle to Establish the World's First Jaguar Preserve.* Washington, D.C.: Island Press, 2000.

In some areas, jaguars enjoy healthy populations, but overall, their numbers continue to decline.

INDEX